Come into His Presence

with Come, We That Love the Lord

Unknown
Arr. by Carol Tornquist

Simply ♩ = ca. 92

4

mel.

mel.

poco rall.   a tempo

mf   rall.

Song ending   Medley ending

*"Come, We That Love the Lord" (Aaron Williams)

Slightly faster ♩ = ca. 104

rit.   p   mf

We Worship and Adore You

with Joyful, Joyful, We Adore Thee

Traditional
Arr. by Carol Tornquist

Slowly, with reverence ♩ = ca. 76

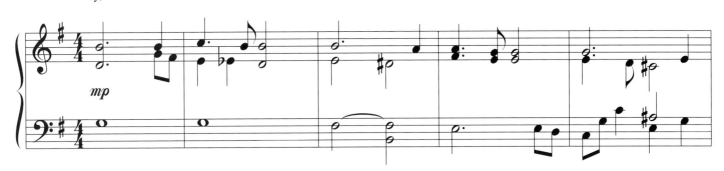

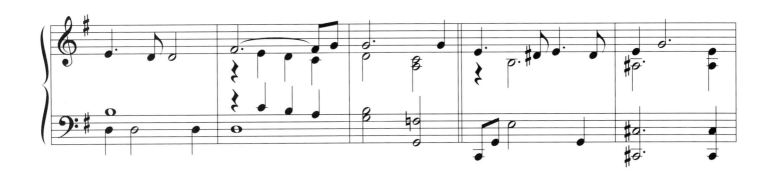

Song ending

Medley ending
Slightly faster ♩ = ca. 92

rit.

*"Joyful, Joyful, We Adore Thee" (Ludwig van Beethoven, from *Ninth Symphony*)

Be Still and Know

with Near to the Heart of God

Anonymous
Arr. by Carol Tornquist

Slowly ♩ = ca. 80

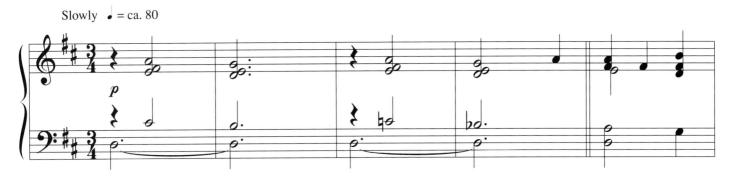

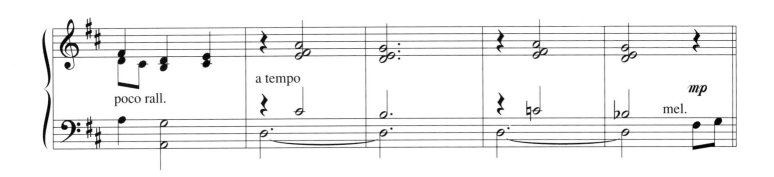

Moderate

12

*"Near to the Heart of God" (Cleland B. McAfee)

Medley ending   Slowly, with expression

Peace Like a River

with Like a River Glorious

Traditional
Arr. by Carol Tornquist

Legato, not too fast ♩ = ca. 72

Song ending

Medley ending

a tempo

poco rit.

*"Like a River Glorious" (James Mountain)

Slightly faster ♩ = ca. 80

mf

Lord, We Praise You

with Praise Him! Praise Him!

OTIS SKILLINGS
Arr. by Carol Tornquist

Gently ♩ = ca. 96

20

*"Praise Him! Praise Him!" (Chester G. Allen)

I Will Sing of the Mercies

with There's a Wideness in God's Mercy

JAMES H. FILLMORE
Arr. by Carol Tornquist

Song ending

Medley ending

rit.

rall.

Moderate Four ♩ = ca. 80

*"There's a Wideness in God's Mercy" (Lizzie S. Tourjee)

Instrument of Worship

with O Worship the King

Unknown
Arr. by Carol Tornquist

28

*"O Worship the King" (From Gardiner's *Sacred Melodies*, 1815)

Jesus Is My Lord

with All Hail the Power of Jesus' Name

Unknown
Arr. by Carol Tornquist

Gently ♩ = ca. 80

*"All Hail the Power of Jesus' Name (Oliver Holden)

a tempo

rall.

a tempo
mel.

Oh, How I Love Jesus

with My Jesus, I Love Thee

Traditional American Melody
Arr. by Carol Tornquist

Flowing ♩ = ca. 112

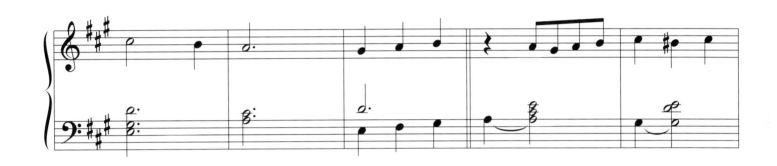

*"My Jesus, I Love Thee" (Adoniram J. Gordon)

Rejoice in the Lord Always

with Rejoice, Ye Pure in Heart

Traditional
Arr. by Carol Tornquist

Moderate two ♩ = ca. 72

*"Rejoice, Ye Pure in Heart" (Arthur H. Messitur)

Blessed Be the Name

with Take the Name of Jesus with You

Unknown
Arr. by Carol Tornquist

Moderate four ♩ = ca. 88

Song ending

Medley ending *"Take the Name of Jesus with You" (William H. Doane)

Slightly slower ♩ = ca. 72

Oh, the Blood of Jesus

with Nothing But the Blood

Unknown
Arr. by Carol Tornquist

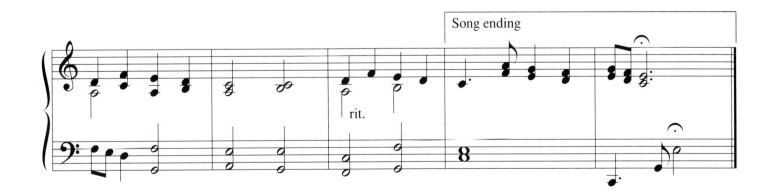

*"Nothing But the Blood" (Robert Lowry)

CONTENTS

MEDLEYS OF Praise

Hymns and Choruses for Solo Piano

Arranged by
CAROL TORNQUIST

Moderately Easy

Lillenas PUBLISHING COMPANY
KANSAS CITY, MO 64141